A FIRST LOOK AT HISTORY

Vikings

by Fiona Macdonald

Consultant: Dr. Richard Hall

GARETH**STEVENS**

GS

P U B L I S H I N G
A WRC Media Company

Please visit our web site at: www.garethstevens.com
For a free color catalog describing Gareth Stevens Publishing's
list of high-quality books and multimedia programs, call
1-800-542-2595 (USA) or 1-800-387-3178 (Canada).
Gareth Stevens Publishing's fax: (414) 332-3567.

Library of Congress Cataloging-in-Publication Data

Macdonald, Fiona.
 Vikings / Fiona Macdonald.
  p. cm. — (A first look at history)
  ISBN 0-8368-4530-7 (lib. bdg.)
  1. Vikings—Juvenile literature. 2. Norsemen—Juvenile literature.
I. Title. II. Series.
DL65.M29   2005
948'.022—dc22   2004059189

This edition first published in 2005 by
Gareth Stevens Publishing
A WRC Media Company
330 West Olive Street, Suite 100
Milwaukee, Wisconsin 53212 USA

This U.S. edition copyright © 2005 by Gareth Stevens, Inc.
Original edition copyright © 2004 by ticktock Entertainment Ltd.
First published in Great Britain in 2005 by ticktock Media Ltd.,
Unit 2, Orchard Business Centre, North Farm Road, Tunbridge
Wells, Kent, TN2 3XF, United Kingdom.

Gareth Stevens series editor: Dorothy L. Gibbs
Gareth Stevens art direction: Tammy West

Picture credits (t=top, b=bottom, c=center, l=left, r=right)
AKG: 5tr. Alamy: 4-5. Graham Collins: 5tl, 12tr, 14, 16l. Corbis: 6-7,
7tr, 7cr, 8, 9r (both), 10-11 (all), 12b, 13l (both), 19l, 19r (both),
20-21. Richard Hall: 21br. Heritage Image Partnership: 17tl.
PB Photo Agency: 9tl. Ticktock: 2-3, 7tl, 13cr, 18l, 21tl, 22-23, 23tr.
Universitetets Oldsaksamling Oslo: 16-17, 17r (all). Werner Forman: 5cr,
7br, 15r (all), 18r, 23br. York Archaeological Trust: 1, 5br, 13br, 15l (all),
21tr, 23bl.

Every effort has been made to trace the copyright holders for the
photos used in this book. The publisher apologizes, in advance, for
any unintentional omissions and would be pleased to insert appropriate
acknowledgments in any subsequent edition of this publication.

Printed in the United States of America

1 2 3 4 5 6 7 8 9 09 08 07 06 05

Contents

Words in the glossary are printed in **boldface** type the first time they appear in the text.

Meet the Vikings

Vikings were fearless explorers and warriors. They sailed from their homes in Norway, Sweden, and Denmark to attack towns and villages all over Europe.

The Vikings were a powerful force in Europe for more than three hundred years, from about AD 800 to 1100. At first, Viking warriors were led by **warlords**. Later, they were ruled by kings.

Vikings were rough and tough, and they loved to argue, but they loved music, dancing, feasting, storytelling, jokes, tricks, and sports, too.

Besides being warriors, Vikings were skillful sailors, busy **traders**, and hardworking farmers. They were fierce, but they also valued fairness and free speech, and they made many laws.

Viking Artifacts

The Vikings were expert shipbuilders. Their longships were made of overlapping wooden planks.

Viking craftworkers carved detailed designs into wood.

The Vikings' musical instruments included wooden **panpipes** and whistles made from swans' leg bones.

Viking Adventures

Sailing on dangerous voyages over stormy seas, Viking explorers hoped to become famous, take over new lands, and get rich. The Vikings loved adventure!

Viking sailors traveled in fast warships, powered by men rowing with oars and by the wind blowing against huge, cloth sails. They did not have maps. They used clouds and the stars to guide them in the right direction.

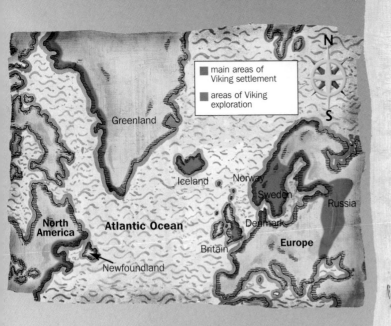

main areas of Viking settlement

areas of Viking exploration

N

S

Greenland

Iceland

Norway

Sweden

Russia

North America

Atlantic Ocean

Denmark

Europe

Britain

Newfoundland

Longships had decorative weather vanes attached to their masts to show Viking sailors which way the wind was blowing.

Sailing west, the Vikings reached Iceland, Greenland, and North America. To reach the **Middle East**, Viking traders traveled overland through Russia. Sometimes, they had to drag their ships on frozen rivers.

The anchor on a Viking ship was a rock. It held the ship in place when it reached a shore.

This bronze **Buddha** statue came to Swedish Vikings from India, after being bought and sold many times along the way.

7

Ruthless Raiders

Viking meant pirate! The first Viking **raiders** sailed from their homelands to make surprise attacks on trading centers and **monasteries** close to the sea. Later, Vikings built camps and settlements in the lands they had won.

Huge, carved monsters were built onto the fronts of Viking ships to frighten people during an attack.

During a Viking raid, no one was safe! Vikings attacked people in churches, monasteries, towns, villages, and on farms.

Actors dressed as Viking raiders.

Viking raiders stole gold and silver and captured people to sell as **slaves**. They grabbed all they could, set fire to whatever remained, then hurried away.

Kings in England and France paid the Vikings money to stop their raiding. This payment, or tax, was called danegeld. When kings refused to pay, the Vikings killed them!

Viking Artifacts

In AD 1018, Viking raiders took 40 tons (37 tonnes) of silver from England as a danegeld payment.

This tombstone shows Viking raiders attacking with swords and battle-axes.

Vikings at Home

Most Viking houses were made of wood and had only one big room, called a hall. Outside their houses, Vikings built sheds for storing food and protecting their animals during cold weather.

Inside, Viking houses were smelly and stuffy. They had dirt floors, and some houses had no windows. Beds were wooden platforms built around the inside walls of the house.

A **reconstruction** of the inside of a Viking house.

The hall of a Viking home had a smoky fire in the middle of the floor. In the evenings, families often listened to stories around the fire.

This building (left) is a reconstruction of a Viking royal building. Experts on Viking history believe it may have been used as a workshop or, possibly, for storage.

Actors showing Viking women at work.

Viking women were in charge of the home. They cooked, took care of the children, and wove cloth to make clothes.

This modern-day house in Iceland was built to look like a Viking home of the past. It is made of stone and **turf**. In places like Iceland, there were no trees, so Vikings built their houses out of stone and turf.

The Vikings used large wooden chests for storing valuables.

Viking Food

The Vikings grew a lot of the food they ate. Farmers plowed fields to plant vegetables, such as cabbages and peas, for eating in soups and stews. Viking farmers also grew oats and **barley**, for making bread and beer.

Viking farmers raised cattle, goats, and sheep. They ate their meat, made cheese from their milk, and used their skins to make leather.

The Vikings ate many wild foods, too. Using bows and arrows, they hunted and killed rabbits; ducks; small birds; wild boars; deer, including reindeer; and even bears. Viking sailors caught seals, walrus, and many kinds of fish to eat.

Viking boys climbed cliffs to trap seabirds and collect their eggs. Girls collected seaweed for food.

Viking Artifacts

Nuts, **herbs**, mushrooms, wild garlic, and berries were some of the wild foods the Vikings gathered from meadows and forests.

Vikings drank from wooden cups and cattle horns.

Querns were pairs of round stones that Vikings rubbed together to grind oats and barley into flour.

Viking Fashion

When it came to clothing, Vikings liked to look good. They chose bright colors for their clothes and trimmed them with fur, **braid**, and embroidery.

Viking men wore **tunics** and trousers. Women wore long dresses, **pinafores**, and shawls. To keep warm, everyone wore hats, boots, and **cloaks**.

Viking men and women both styled their hair and wore homemade makeup.

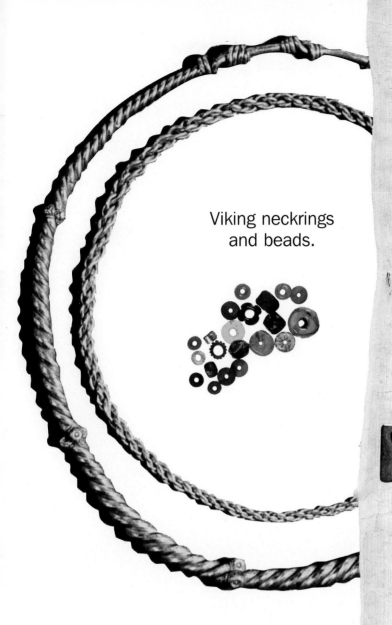

Viking neckrings
and beads.

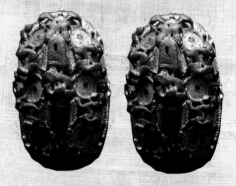

Viking women often wore
pairs of brooches, fastening
one brooch to their clothing
at each shoulder.

Vikings smoothed their
long hair with combs made
out of bone or deer antlers.

The Vikings fastened clothing
such as cloaks with beautiful
brooches made of gold, silver,
and other metals. They wore
a lot of jewelry, including rings,
bracelets, and bead necklaces.

Warriors were given **ornate**
metal armbands as rewards
for fighting bravely. They wore
the armbands with pride!

Deadly Weapons

Vikings valued courage more than life itself. Viking men joined armies led by kings and warlords, whom they followed loyally. Warriors fought bravely, hoping to win high honor and praise and be remembered long after they had died.

Viking warriors fought with bows and arrows, battle-axes, spears, and swords. They protected their bodies by wearing tunics of padded leather and carrying wooden shields. Some Viking chiefs and top warriors wore **chain mail** armor.

A berserker warrior chess piece.

Viking warriors gave their favorite swords vicious names, such as Sharp Biter or Viper, which is the name of a deadly snake.

Berserker warriors worked themselves into a state of **rage** before a battle. They dressed in bearskin cloaks, ground their teeth, chewed their shields, then fought furiously!

The Vikings were famous for fighting with battle-axes. The metal heads on these weapons were so sharp they could slice through armor.

Warriors wore heavy, metal helmets to protect their heads. The helmets had nose guards and protective strips around the eyes.

Spears were for throwing long distances, as Vikings tried to stop enemies who were trying to escape.

Gods and Heroes

Because the Vikings believed that gods ruled the world, they **sacrificed** dogs, horses, and even people to please their gods.

Thor was the god of thunderstorms. The Vikings believed that he made lightning flash across the sky. Thor was big and very strong — but not very smart!

A bronze statue of Thor.

Warrior goddesses called Valkyries carried the souls of dead Viking heroes to Valhalla, a great Viking hall in the sky. At Valhalla, the heroes fought all day and feasted all night.

Odin was the greatest Viking god. He was a brave and clever god who brought victory in battle.

For good luck, Vikings wore **charms** shaped like Thor's mighty hammer.

A Viking picture stone showing Odin riding his magic horse.

As Odin rode his magic, eight-legged horse across the sky, two **ravens** flew beside him. The names of the ravens were "Thought" and "Memory."

This tombstone is carved with spiky letters called **runes**. Vikings believed that runes had magic powers.

Living in New Lands

Over the years, many Vikings left their homelands and looked for new places to live. Some wanted to find better farmland. Others wanted to run their own lives, away from the power of new Viking kings.

Vikings settled in Scotland, England, Ireland, France, Iceland, and Greenland. Vikings, called Rus, settled in eastern Europe, in the land still known today as Russia.

A Viking named Leif Eriksson was the first European to land in North America. He arrived at Newfoundland in about AD 1000.

The Vikings who settled in North America fought among themselves, as well as with the Native Americans, and left after only a few years.

Viking Settlements

A Viking settlement was discovered at York, in England. This picture shows **archaeologists** digging up Viking **remains**.

This building is a modern reconstruction of one of the buildings from the Viking settlement in North America.

The Vikings Today

Many Viking words are still used today in lands where the Vikings once settled. Viking words in the English language include *birth*, *deaf*, *egg*, *fang*, *freckle*, *knife*, *ship*, and *sky*.

Archaeologists have found many Viking burial mounds. When **excavated**, they tell us about life in Viking times.

This longship was found under a large mound in a field at Oseberg, in Norway. A Viking queen and her servant girl were buried inside.

Some Viking activities, such as skiing and ice-skating, are still very popular today. Viking hunters used skis to chase animals across snowy ground.

Vikings crossed frozen lakes wearing ice skates made from animal bones.

Viking Artifacts

← **Birsay A 967**

Many places in the world still have Viking names. Birsay, on the Orkney Islands, means "hunting ground island" in the Viking language.

Some days of the week are named after Viking gods. Thursday is named for Thor. Friday is named for Freyja, the goddess of love.

A Viking **pendant** showing Freyja.

Glossary

archaeologists: people who dig up objects that help them study history

barley: a type of grain

berserker: a very fierce Viking warrior

braid: decorative rope or cord made of threads or fabric wound together

brooches: pieces of jewelry pinned to clothing as fasteners or decoration

Buddha: a statue of Gautama Buddha, who founded the Buddist religion

chain mail: a type of armor made up of thousands of small metal rings that are linked as if woven together

charms: trinkets or ornaments that are miniature animals, people, or objects

cloaks: sleeveless coats, or capes

excavated: dug up

herbs: sweet-smelling plants used to flavor foods and to make medicines

Middle East: an area of the world that includes parts of Africa, Asia and Europe and countries such as Egypt, Israel, Saudi Arabia, and Turkey

monasteries: places where holy men called monks live, work, and pray

ornate: very fancy and decorative

panpipes: groups of short tubes that make flutelike sounds when air is blown into them

pendant: a type of necklace that is usually a charm hanging from a chain

pinafores: sleeveless, full-length aprons that are worn over dresses

rage: violent anger

raiders: unfriendly invaders who make sudden and unexpected attacks

ravens: large, black birds that Vikings believed ate the flesh of dead warriors

reconstruction: something built to look the same as it would have earlier in history

remains: things left behind

runes: the characters of a mysterious ancient European alphabet

ruthless: without care or concern for the pain and suffering of others

sacrificed: killed as an offering to gods

slaves: captured people who are sold to work as servants

traders: people who make a living by buying, selling, and exchanging goods

tunics: long shirts that look like sleeveless dresses

turf: thick mats of soil held together by grass and roots

warlords: powerful men who were good at fighting and led their own private armies